5/16

The Eighth Grade Millionaire

The Eighth Grade Millionaire

By Edward R. Mercer

Dedication

This book is dedicated to my loving mother and my youngest brother. Before my mother passed away she made me promise I would one day write a book. This is me keeping my promise. And to my brother who passed away at twelve years old with leukemia. His dying words were, "If I were to grow, as an adult I would want to be just like you." I hope I did not let him down.

Table of Contents

Chapter One

In the Beginning

Life is a gift, and it's time you unwrapped it.

I am going to begin this book by asking you to complete all of your projects large and small. Clear your desk and your mind of past projects and let's get on with achieving your dream. It is your responsibility to be the best you can be. No one else is responsible for that, and no one else can help you unless you help yourself. No matter how young or how old you are, look to your past experiences to develop a new attitude about your future and your outlook on life.

I have spent a lot of time in France. I was once asked if I had ever had a French kiss. I smiled and said, "No, I only give the girls Australian kisses. It's similar to a French kiss but it's just a little more down under. I know the spot on a woman's body that will drive her crazy." The gentleman who asked this became excited and intrigued. He asked if I could share this information with him. I told him my secret. "It is the heart."

You will find that I throw these zingers into the pages of the book every so often but it is not without intent. I truly do believe a person's heart is one of the most powerful tools in becoming successful. You need someone on your journey in life who you can trust, go to for anything and to rely on. This may not be someone you are romantically involved with. It could be a best friend or a business partner. What I want people to realize is that we are not alone on our path in life. Although we are the only one's who are responsible for our life, we never need to take the journey alone.

You are the main character in this book. It is not about me. It refers to my life experiences and what I have learned in life in order to share with you what you can do to realize your dreams. Without action no idea you have can be transformed into reality. The most successful people I have come across all have one thing in common. They were all incredibly determined. Staying power is incredibly important.

The people who quit at the first sign of difficulty will never achieve their goals.

You have probably read this in several books or been told this by several people in your life: Do not underestimate the power of positive thinking. When I was a young man I got my hand caught in a steel grinder. I was rushed to the hospital and after many doctors looked at my hand they said they would not be able to save it. I refused to believe it. Over one hundred stitches later they managed to salvage my hand, however, they told me I would never be able to regain its use. Again, I refused to believe it. I carried about a rubber ball all day every day and squeezed it as tightly as I could. At first I was weak but gradually I built up strength. I am now able to shake hands with everyone I meet, and they are none the wiser I had an accident where I almost lost my hand. It was because of the power of positive thinking. I did not believe for a second I was going to lose my hand, and, therefore, I didn't. You have the ability to choose your outlook on life. Allow that outlook to be positive, and positive things will happen for you.

I worked in a factory in shipping in receiving. After my eight-hour shift I would walk across the street and begin another eight-hour shift as a bellboy at the Holiday Inn. I worked tirelessly to provide for myself. One night on my way home from work, I was attacked by a group of men. They broke my nose and dislocated my shoulder before robbing me of every penny I had. I was taken to the hospital and scheduled for an operation to mend my shoulder. As I lay in bed that night, I tried to figure out how I was going to pay for the hospital expenses. I decided to tie my belt around my shoulder and pull it back into its socket. I left the hospital that night and, having no money for a taxi, I walked twelve miles to my home. The next day I was back working my regular sixteen-hour workday. I was in pain, but I fought through it to complete my tasks.

One of my colleagues approached me to commend me on how tough I was. He said that with my tolerance to pain I should take up kickboxing. I had never entertained the idea but after he put the bug in my ear, I went on to train and become a national champion. I won fifteen out of sixteen matches by first round knockouts. I took a negative occurrence in my life and turned it into a positive experience that shaped much of who I am today. I will share stories like these throughout the book to remind you that roadblocks should never get in the way of achieving your end goal. I have dealt with many hardships and I have never allowed them to obstruct my path to success.

The human brain weighs about three pounds and occupies about ninety cubic inches in your skull. Your brain transmits messages through your electrochemical system, which informs you of the universe that surrounds you. Your brain receives information as electrical signals pouring in from your eyes, ears, nose, mouth, and fingertips. The neurons in your brain can simultaneously process and interpret these signals. It then stores all of the information it collects for later. Are you starting to see the picture I am painting? Your brain is complex and it does not miss a beat. You must feed your brain positive messages because it will in turn store these massages for later. If you allow your mind to collect negativity, you waste space that might have received positive messages.

Ask yourself this: How strong is your desire to succeed? You must have enough personal desire and determination to succeed or this book will not help in the least. You must have enough strength to pursue your goals without getting off track. You must be able to accept setbacks and turn them into opportunities for yourself. If you believe that you can do all of these things, then you are ready to pursue your goals and become successful.

You have been given a second chance to get it right. Most people are not given that gift. Use it wisely.

Chapter Two

Unfortunate Circumstances Present Opportunity

In determining what it is that defines success and failure in a person, many often wonder, is it a gene or maybe the lifestyle one grew up in? Was there a pivotal point in one's childhood or adulthood that led to their success or failure? Were the planets aligned at the certain time of one's birth? Theories upon theories have been developed to try to explain why some individuals end up successful and others don't.

For me, I have come to understand an enduring formula. My experience has shown me that all kinds of people from many different cultures, lifestyles, and ages have become exceptionally successful. These men and women, myself included, are in a league of individuals who have caught the dream and refuse to let go. Genes and lifestyles aside, when you persevere to reach your goal no matter what, you will confidently succeed.

One of the most important keys to success is to not allow any excuses to prevent you from reaching your full potential. Let me be your example of someone who did not allow my childhood to determine my success or failure in life. I persevered in many aspects of my life and created my own pivotal moments to become who I am today.

My very loving mother gave birth to me when she was a mere fifteen years of age. She was a simple, uneducated farm girl who was swept off her feet by a handsome man. My father, however endearing, was not a responsible man. He was abusive and neglected his familial duties. He married my mother out of obligation and never treated her the way she deserved to be treated. He brought her to Buffalo, New York for their honeymoon. My mother had never been to the United States, nor had she ever stayed in a hotel room before. This was meant to be a memorable moment in her life. Upon arrival my father told her he was going out to buy cigarettes. She waited three days without money or food, not knowing if he would ever return. When he did return, he admitted that he had been on a drunken binge with another woman for three days. My mother loved unconditionally. She stayed with my father.

Shortly after I was born my mother became pregnant with her second child and then her third. She had a total of five children without the means to properly care for us. I used to think to myself that our house had been decorated by a hurricane. We moved a lot because rent payments were due so home never really felt like home. My father continued on his drunken binges, oftentimes bringing women home with him. It was a less than desirable atmosphere to grow up in, but it was all we had.

When I was four years old I became very ill due to lack of nutrition. I was riddled with worms and I had large boils covering the surface of my body. My face became so inflamed that I lost my eyesight for a period of time. However unfair, to be so young and yet feel like you will not live to see another day is empowering. It gave me the strength to realize that if I overcame my illness, I could triumph in life. I was given a second chance.

My grandparents volunteered to take me in. My grandmother saved my life. She covered my body in poultices to draw out the poison and infection. She stayed by my side watching over me and sleeping beside me seven days a week for three months. She taught me that unconditional love and patience can triumph even the greatest trials.

When I regained my health I was old enough to attend school. Unfortunately, halfway through my first year I again fell ill. I was diagnosed with pneumonia and was bedridden for several months. When I felt well enough to try to leave my bed, my arches collapsed and I lost the motor skills in my legs. I required specialty shoes that were astronomically expensive. My grandparents spent their entire life savings on giving me the gift of being able to walk again. They once again taught me that money is just a material factor. Love and determination is more powerful than anything money has to offer.

I was living comfortably with my grandparents when my father happened upon information about

Baby Bonuses. He realized that parents were entitled to money from the government if they had their children living under the same roof. He forced his parents to allow me to return home. My father put me to work at a nearby farm where he would drop me off at 7:00 am and pick me up at 5:00 pm. I would work tirelessly picking tomatoes, strawberries, and apples to earn an income. My father would pick me up from work and collect the money I had made. Greed kills all beauty. I worked hard for myself and my father's greed shrouded me in bitter anger and resentment.

Life presents you with many ups and downs. There are hard days and even harder days. Sometimes you may feel like your life cannot get any worse. I know this feeling and, unfortunately, life continuously presents us with trials we must learn to overcome.

After a few short months of living with my parents, my father began to come home drunk. He would beat my mother for no reason and then come into my room and sexually assault me. I was afraid to fall asleep at night because I knew he would break into my room and repeatedly rape me. I contemplated ending my life many times. I thought it would end the pain I was experiencing, but then I also thought about my grandparents. They fought for me, provided for me, and gave me a second chance. Love can triumph pain. I truly believe you can overcome anything when you consider love for one's self, love for others, and the love people possess for you.

It wasn't until one of my teachers saw the blood from my beatings seeping through my t-shirt at school one day. She reported it to the authorities and I was able to legally return to my grandparent's home. I had made it through another trial in my life. I was alive and I was given the opportunity to accomplish great things in my life.

The next time you're in your vehicle notice this: The rearview mirror is small. It only shows you what's behind you, what has come to pass in your life. The windshield is big. It presents you with a clear view of the future. One must continue to look forward to the things that lie ahead. Do not continue to look into the rearview mirror and contemplate things past. Look forward and realize your potential to do great things.

I am going to share with you something that has the potential to change your life forever. Your willingness to seize this opportunity will allow you become a stronger person. I want you to summon your courage and contact the one person in your life who has affected you negatively. Whether this person has stolen from you, lied to you, verbally abused, or sexually assaulted you, you need to pick up the phone and call this person. You need to tell them that what they have done to you has been on your mind and that you forgive them. You cannot move forward into your future if you are living in the past.

Life is not a rehearsal. You need to give it your best shot. If we spend our whole life living in the past and dwelling on the unfortunate, we may miss the fortunate opportunities that present themselves. I have come to discover something important in life. Whether we are rich or poor, fortunate or unfortunate, we have the same sixty seconds in every minute, the same twenty-four hours in every day and the same 365 days in every year. It is what we do in the time that is allotted to us that's important.

Do not spend this time on negative thoughts and feelings. Forgive and move on. I forgave my father. He taught me hatred and resentment but he also taught me the power to be strong. Without the tribulations he put me through, I may never have discovered the drive to fight and move forward in life. Nothing is worth dwelling in the past. Look through your front windshield and move forward.

We cannot be successful without some element of risk involved. Most people never move forward because all they think about is what if it doesn't work out. My accountant asked me what if it doesn't work out and I replied, what if it does.

Chapter Three

Keep Negativity Out of Your Life

My mother was a powerful influence in my life. Her strength and determination taught me a lot about being strong in the face of adversity. She had many sayings. Some were clever and thoughtful, others were funny and whimsical. I vividly remember one afternoon when I was mowing the lawn and my mother was annoyed with me for not wearing shoes while doing my chores. She yelled to me from across the yard, "If you cut your feet off, don't come running to me." Her sense of humor and caring temperament still make me smile to this day. She said some things I did not agree with. She once told me that what you don't know will hurt you and what you do know will hurt you tremendously. I now know that this statement can be very damaging to one's growth as a person.

Knowledge is wealth. I would personally give up a good meal in place of a good book. I truly believe that next to balancing our bankbooks, knowledge is our next currency. We must open our minds to the wealth of knowledge before us and embrace what we can learn from others and ourselves.

I have had many people over the years tell me that this is easier for me than it is for them. I have access to advisors. I have people to teach me and advise me in how to become successful. The truth is that I do have a board of directors; they just so happen to be Napoleon Hill, Jim Rohn, Zig Ziglar, and the list goes on.

I have learned from most notarized men and women in their field. These men and women have never known they sit on my board of directors. I have been taught by the best because I read their books and I listen to their motivational tapes. When someone asks me, how far is it from London, Ontario to Toronto? I respond: "One tape." And from Toronto to Windsor? "Four tapes." We can learn an absolute wealth of knowledge from those whom we look up to and our peers. We all come from different backgrounds and we all have distinctive careers, strengths, and weaknesses. By learning from each other and doing what we can to help others, we can become great individuals.

Everything I listen to is positive. I have no space in my head or in my heart for negativity. Life is like an echo. Whatever you put out into the universe you will get back. Echoes do not lie nor do they exaggerate. An echo is 100 percent a reflection of what you say and do. If you exude rudeness, arrogance, and negativity, you will be sure to attract the same negative energy in return. If you put out positive vibes, love, and affection, the same rules apply. You will most definitely attract beautiful and warm personality types. We all need to make a conscious effort to be positive. Whether we are having a good day or maybe we are down on our luck, being positive is the only way to overcome adversity.

I have been fortunate to meet identical twin brothers who have taught me a lot about the effects of being positive and negative in life. The first brother I met had a very negative attitude. He failed to see the good moments in life and choose to relive the bad moments. He had been unfortunate enough to fall under the influence of drugs and alcohol. He did not see the good in what would come if he tried to beat his addictions. When I asked him about his demeanor, he responded aggressively. He told me that he came from a very poor upbringing. His father was an alcoholic who also fell victim to drug abuse. He would beat him and his brother with no remorse for his actions. This twin had the attitude that his upbringing made him who he is today and nothing was going to change that.

A short time later, I was introduced to the second of the two brothers. He was dressed impeccably and arrived to a dinner party in a stunning black Mercedes. He was the top attorney at this firm and was known by everyone as an all around, wonderful person. I complimented him on his kind demeanor and asked him how he became so successful. He responded that he came from a meager background. His father was an alcoholic and drug abuser who beat him and his brother. However, his perspective on life was that negativity robs us of all the positive gifts life has to offer. He chose to block out negativity and to not allow his upbringing to prevent him from accomplishing great things in life.

After meeting the twin brothers and witnessing the power of positive thinking I had to ask myself, am I doing all that I can to remain positive and to live out the good moments in life while avoiding the negatives? Each of us will be somewhere in the next twelve months. The million-dollar question is: Where will you be if you continue on the path that you have been following for the past twelve months? It is what you do on a daily basis that will determine your future and what will give you long-term positive results.

The longest journey in life always begins with the first step. If you have read this and have had to question whether you are truly happy with the path you are on right now, you may need to consider altering your path. Success is the result of your achievements. Do not settle in the path you are on if what you want has not yet been achieved. Abundance in life is directly correlated with how negative or how positive you are in your endeavors. Always have a positive mindset and think big when it comes to your endeavors.

It is my belief that no one can achieve great things in life if they settle for anything less than greatness. And lastly, do not be standing at the airport while you are waiting for your ship to come in. Realize your mistakes, seize the opportunities before you, and dream big because how successful you will become is reflected in the standards you set for yourself and the positive outlook you shed on all opportunities.

When warning signs are evident, do not ignore them. If a project or opportunity starts out with negativity or skepticism, chances are the project might fail. Proceed with caution and you will be better for it.

Chapter Four

Turn Negativity into Opportunity

A very dear friend of mine once told me never to ask someone to do something I haven't ever done myself. In telling you to pick up the phone to call someone who has wronged you in the past or to keep negativity out of your life and defeat adversity with a positive attitude, I am trying to motivate you in ways that have been effective for me. The twin brothers mentioned in the last chapter taught me that one's past can shape one's life positively or negatively depending on how one lets past circumstances affect them. I am now asking you to turn any negative experiences in your life into a learning curve and to challenge yourself to engage in something that turns negativity into opportunity.

When I was thirteen years old I was involved in activities I am not proud of. I was hanging out with men who were decades older and I was willing to engage in anything to be accepted. I was smoking, drinking, and fighting people for next to no reason because I wanted to fit in. This is seemingly the classic story of a street kid trying to find somewhere to belong. The problem with my situation is that I was not homeless. I was still living with my grandparents who were providing me with a promising future.

By the time I turned sixteen I had been in and out of juvenile detention centers on a few separate occasions. On one particular occasion I was in court and the judge happened to know my grandfather very well. The judge asked me one simple question that evoked a lot of emotion. I never cried. It was instilled in me that it was not manly to cry, but this simple question broke me to tears. He asked me if I loved my grandfather. I knew I loved my grandfather very much. I also knew he was asking me this for the simple reason I was letting down someone whom I loved very much. Upon hearing the news of my arrest, my grandfather had a heart attack.

This moment changed my life forever. I never again wanted to be the source of heartbreak and disappointment. I took my negative past and turned it into a wonderful opportunity. I began working with an organization called Scared Straight. I was a mediator for troubled youth who had seemingly lost their way. Many of the children I worked with were in and out of juvenile detention centers, much like myself, and the next stop for them would be prison if they did not acknowledge the wrong in their actions and try to turn themselves around. I found I was able to get through to these children because I was once in their shoes. I was not asking them to do something I myself hadn't already done.

I went from working with Scared Straight to volunteering for the Suicide Hotline and then to an association which assisted battered housewives. I enjoyed volunteering and continuously saw the positive outcomes I was making in others' lives as well as my own. I went on to work for the John Howard Association, which was designed to assist men who were previously in prison and who were unable to get a job due to their criminal records. My volunteer experience was rewarding and oftentimes breathtaking. It made me want to make a better life for myself and those around me.

After many years of working for volunteer organizations, I realized I needed to further my career in paid work. One thing that never ceases to amaze me about life is that it is full of opportunity. Whether those opportunities are born of positivity or negativity, everyone has the same potential to seize an opportunity and turn it into something amazing. Here is where I will share my first step in becoming a millionaire: When applying for positions I would tell the employer I did not want an hourly wage, I wanted to be paid solely on commission. My reason being that when someone is paid hourly, they are not earning what they are worth, they are earning what someone else thinks they are worth. Getting paid hourly also puts a proverbial ceiling on your earnings, which is the first step in limiting your possibilities.

I began my career in sales by selling magazine subscriptions, encyclopedias, vacuum cleaners, home improvements, and more. I was willing to take any opportunity that came my way and because of that I thrived in sales positions. Many people believe that being a successful salesperson requires training and skill. It is my personal opinion it requires determination and a willingness to succeed.

I walked into a shopping mall one afternoon and happened upon a couple of men who were selling black velvet paintings. I enquired whether or not they sold wholesale and although it was not something they had tried in the past, I convinced them of the opportunity and they agreed to sell their paintings at wholesale prices for me to resell.

Within the first day of purchasing the paintings, I had sold my stock and was interested in acquiring exclusivity with their product. I invested every penny I had into the paintings and obtained an exclusive deal with the artist. I began selling the paintings on street corners and, as luck would have it, this is where I met a man who already sold products in Kmart. He asked me if I would be interested in working with him and, upon agreeing, we were given the center aisle in over eighty Canadian stores. I was making more money in a single week than many people make in many months, if not a full year.

Life is what you make of it. You must turn all experiences, whether negative or positive, into opportunities. Do not limit yourself in anything you do. The sky is the limit so why put a ceiling over your head? Do not allow past circumstances to affect your growth and development as a person. Seize every moment and turn it into learning experience. It took the love of my family for me to realize that I was only creating negative experiences for myself. My family's love also taught me to turn negativity into opportunity, which is how I ended up in volunteer work and, ultimately, in sales. You never know where opportunity will take you, so seize it and make it your next success in life.

If the system has failed us it is time for us to take our chestnuts out of the fire. Neither the government nor anyone else is responsible for us. We must take care of ourselves. That is why I am writing this book. I want to give you insight and inspiration to help guide you.

Chapter Five
1440 Minutes

Everyday, rich or poor, we have 1440 minutes and 86,400 ticks of the clock to make something happen in our day. Millionaires are not extraordinary people; millionaires are people who do extraordinary things. They set goals and they make every moment of every day count.

I truly believe that riches begin with thoughts. Both wealth and poverty are a form of thought. If you believe you were dealt a hand in life and you are satisfied with it, you will never strive to become more then what you currently are. I was a street person at the age of fifteen. My grandparents worked hard to provide for me, however, when they passed away, I did not have the means to sustain the house. I was on the streets with no food, clean clothing, or the resources to get myself off the streets. If I allowed myself to believe that this is what life was offering me, I never would have become the person I am today. A quitter never wins, and a winner never quits. I did not give up on myself and I found opportunity in the most obscure places because I did not give up and I put passion and drive into all of my endeavors.

Canada hosts a "One of a Kind" show in several provinces throughout the year. At one show in particular I met a man who was selling bobbing woodpeckers. He was passionate about his product and although he admitted the product was silly, he appreciated the simplicity of it. After seeing his passion for something so simple and his disappointment in the lack of the success of his product, it was hard to resist wanting to help him. I purchased the remainder of the woodpeckers and because I already had distribution with Kmart, it was easy to convince them to allow me to put the woodpeckers at all of the cash registers. Within two days I had sold 5000 units and the demand was continuous. I was proud to be helping a man who showed passion in his product. I felt accomplished in creating a market phenomenon out of a product that was unlikely to take off in such a capacity.

I cannot deny that small-scale business ventures are where I began my career. Being involved in the sale of market trend items taught me the value of believing in the product I was selling and the importance of passion and drive. I was once told that 80 percent of success is mindset. You have to find your gift in life and share it with as many people as you can. My gift was the ability to sell and to help others along the way. This led me to my next business venture, which was multi-level marketing.

The Competition Bureau of Canada defines multi-level marketing as a plan for the distribution of products whereby participants earn money by supplying products to other participants in the same plan. They, in turn, make their money by supplying the same products to other participants. While many people outside of the multi-level marketing industry (and those in it who have tried and failed) will have their biased opinion of multi-level marketing, I believe in it 100 percent. It is truly an endeavor where you get out what you put in. Multi-level marketing takes advantage of passive residual income as well as leverage. Both of these terms are important and yet commonly misunderstood.

Passive residual income is simply income that continues to come to you long after the work you have done to produce it has ended. Multi-level marketing allows you to earn residual income for your hard work and effort and it is truly reflective of the amount of work you put into your investment.

Although not all investments will turn into residual income, if you invest yourself in a product that is highly consumable, meaning that people will want to purchase the product month after month because of its high quality and high demand, then you are sure to see a return on your investment long after the initial work you put into it.

What I deem to be a second major component to multi-level marketing is that it enables you to use leverage to advance yourself and others. I do not want you to hear the word leverage and associate it with leveraging other people to get what you want. Multi-level marketing simply understands that there are only twenty-four hours in a day. One must realize that it does not matter how talented you are or how much effort you put into an endeavor, if you do not take advantage of leverage, you are limited to the number of hours in a day. With the small network of people in a multi-level marketing organization you can produce tremendous results, equivalent to working twenty-four hours in a day, with only a fraction of the individual effort. It is important to understand you are not making other people work for you and leveraging their results, you are working with others in a network to produce results while everyone reaps the rewards of what they put into it.

With that being said, I found my gift was in multi-level marketing because I was willing to pour tremendous amounts of effort into my investment and worked hard to see my efforts turn into wealth. I happened upon multi-level marketing when I was invited to a seminar that was designed to explain the concept of the multi-level marketing system. After the seminar, I walked up to the stage, introduced myself to the president, vice-president, and the members of the audience and explained that I was going to be the number one distributor in their company. They scoffed as they already had thousands of people in the company who had been with them for many years but I knew this was where the wealth of my talents could be put to use.

The night of the seminar was my first night with the company. By the time I was with the company for two months, I had already reached the position as the number one distributor. I was making thousands of dollars each month and although it was not without hard work and determination, I turned my marketing talents into a wealthy investment. This goes to show that everyone has talents and that once those talents are utilized you can achieve anything in life. I went from being homeless in the eighth grade to a millionaire by the time I was twenty-seven because of my efforts in multi-level marketing. The reason why multi-level marketing is dependent upon networking is because the word "work" is very important. Put effort into what you set out to do and you will not be disappointed with the results.

I have been in sales for many years. Whether my business ventures found me in multi-level marketing or whether I was developing property in Costa Rica, I have always been involved in sales in one way or another. It has provided for me very well. If I found my finances struggling, my first remedy would be to find something to sell. Every good business relies on selling and, although many people do not find themselves to be good at sales, we all have the capacity to sell. When I first began in sales I lived by fives does and five don'ts that helped me to excel. Let me share them with you in the hope they may assist you in future endeavors.

It is important to develop a five-foot rule. If someone comes within five feet of you, you should intend to talk to him or her. Strike up a conversation about what they are wearing or the weather. Interaction and networking are vital to successful relationships. This also leads into the next step, which is to learn a few anecdotal stories to break the ice. Once you have started a conversation, a great story is helpful in keeping the attention of your prospect. It is even better if you can develop a story that centers around what you intend to sell. Thirdly, keep yourself up to date on current events. There is nothing worse than not being able to respond to a question regarding current events. People love humor and even more so, they love the person who can make them laugh. Jokes are great. However, it is important to keep them short, clean, and unbiased. Finally, be yourself and do not force a sale. People want to know you, not who you think you should be. Beside, people can oftentimes tell when you are faking it, so why try? Be unique and authentic. Your first interaction with a prospect will be when they get to know you and develop a trusting relationship with you. Do not try to sell them on someone you are not.

There are many don'ts in sales. These are the few I have come to live by. Do not speak about religion or politics. In sales it is very important to remain somewhat neutral. I am not suggesting you should ever downplay your beliefs, simply do not make it a primary topic. You can easily lose the prospective of your client if you launch into a heavy conversation on religion or politics. It is also important to never talk yourself out of a sale. Never underestimate whoever it is you're talking to and remember it is not always about who they are, but rather who they know. To be successful in sales you should never sell. Yes, you read that correctly. In your first encounter with someone, you should never try to sell them something. The first meeting is about you and getting to know them. Finally, do not lie or exaggerate. Need I say more? I have said it once and I will say it again, integrity is the most important framework for any successful business. There is no need to lie or exaggerate and it will never benefit you in sales.

Here is one more tip. You may laugh when you hear this but this tactic made me a lot of money in the world of sales. My business card is round in shape and on the front of my card it says, "To it." When I was a young man selling products door to door, I would do my sales presentation and if a client gave me a negative response to the product I was trying to sell I would respond, "So what you are saying is that you will buy my product when you get around to it?" Most of the time they would say yes and that is when I would hand them my round business card with "To it" on the front. I would go into my presentation once again and most people, impressed with my wit and personality, would hear me out and see my perspective on the product I was selling differently. It was a simple tactic but it worked wonders for me. We all have little quirks and if we can find a way to work them into our sales tactic, we will become all the more successful.

Do you have more now than you did five years ago? If not it may be time to change your ways. Read different books, listen to different motivational tapes, and never play the blame card.

Chapter Six
You Are the Main Character

You are the main character in this book. You are the only person who needs to realize you have the power to change or excel in the circumstances of your life. There are many people in your life who will provoke you and push your buttons. Allow me to provoke you to change the inopportune things in your life. Allow this book to be your blueprint to positive thinking. A blueprint of your dreams if you will, so that when you finish reading it you will have a realization of the things holding you back and you will be determined to change those things for the better.

This book is not to impress you, it is to impress upon you that you and only you have the power to alter your life for the better. I am not suggesting that upon reading this book you will have self-realization and everything will get better. I am suggesting that each time you read this book you may have a sense of enlightenment or a new take on a situation so that it can be turned into opportunity. Sometimes it simply takes a thought-provoking moment to launch us into paths in our life that will change the way we are forever.

A few years ago I was conducting a seminar on millionaire training and how to become wealthy by utilizing the tools your mind provides you with. I got to the stage and looked out over the audience and began to cry. I had the realization that although I may have been successful in assisting people in realize their wealth of opportunities, I was not successful in making those people better than they originally were. Men and women who did not drink became alcoholics. People who did not do drugs ran with a new affluent crowd and began to partake in drugs. What one must realize is that wealth is not measured in financial terms. It does not mean your townhouse must become a penthouse, or your Pontiac a Cadillac. Wealth may be measured in the love you posses and share with others, or the wealth of your thoughts that you can share with others to assist them in becoming more.

Let me share with you the mistake I made when I started to become financially wealthy. I had a beautiful wife and two beautiful children. I gave my wife a beautiful home to live in and a luxury car to drive. She had access to credit cards to go shopping and pamper her and the children with but the one thing my family was missing was the love from me that they deserved. I was doing seminars on how to advance yourself and your career and all the while, I was failing to realize my own family was slipping away from me. How can you help others without realizing the flaws in your own life? How can you ask people to alter the path they are taking without realizing you may be going down the wrong path? It begins with you. You must realize where life is taking you and alter that destination if it is not what will make you truly happy.

My wife and I separated. My children were going to the best school and dressing in the finest clothing, but they grew up not knowing their father or receiving the love they truly deserved. I am sharing this with you because I realized the mistake I had made and only then was I able to help myself and help others to realize they do not have to make the same mistake. Wealth should be measured in love. Money is simply a magnifier of what you already have. Do not allow it to destroy what you have. Allow it to make you a better person and to make a positive difference to those around you.

I am not suggesting for a moment that life is easy and that telling yourself that you will always try to do the right thing for your family is a foolproof plan to a successful marriage. If life were that easy, everyone would be successful. There is a saying that two can live for the price of one. I have come to find that this saying does not hold true for an elephant and a canary who happen to live together. I personally think it is best to view yourself as equal to those around you, as though you are two elephants or two canaries under the same roof. Whether you are a ditch digger, a schoolteacher, or the president of a large corporation, you are contributing something to the community in which you live. All of those contributions can have equal impact on the people around you, so why not consider yourself equal amongst others.

A second thought that my dear mother had me realize at a very young age is that you should never enter into a situation where you plan to loose. Why would you enter a casino and tell yourself that after loosing $200 you are going to go home? You have already predetermined you will not go home successful. My mother would go to the bingo hall and tell me that once she lost her $20 she would come home. I'm glad that she lost every once in a while because again she taught me that entering into a situation where you are prepared to loose will always end in a situation where we are defeated.

If we entered into our marriages or our careers like that, where would our paths lead us? We would be predetermining failure in our life's path. I have never entered into a situation in my life where I planned to lose. Do not set yourself up for that type of failure. Always plan to win and if your situation does not seem to be turning out as a triumphant one, then change that situation into a more positive opportunity. You are the leader in your own life and no leader ever begins a mission with failure in their heart and mind. Do not allow your mission to begin this way either.

The bigger the problem, the bigger the pay check. I found in my life that anything that came too easily never worked out. If it were too easy to succeed, everyone would be successful.

Chapter Seven

Important Things to Live By

When I began writing this book, I knew it was of the utmost importance for me to convey some of the fundamental things I have come to live by. First and foremost is the importance of honesty, faith, love, and integrity. You can take material things away from a person but you can never take away faith, love, and integrity. In order to be successful, you cannot fall short in any one of these things. Ability is important, however, dependability is critical and without it, your abilities will fall short.

I am an incredibly dependable person. It was one of the first things I learnt the importance of, and to this day I do not allow myself to fall short in being dependable. I can proudly boast I have never been late for an appointment. If I am fifteen minutes early, I am on time. It is my belief that if you do not respect a person's time then you do not respect them. If someone tells me they are running behind I do not believe them. If they were running, they wouldn't be late. Lead by example and always strive to be the person that people can always count on. It is an admirable quality and will serve you well in life.

Feeding our good habits is one of the most important principals we can live by. In doing so, you will stall your bad habits and allow for more positivity in your life. There was a guy who said, "I do not know how to spell procrastination but I will look it up tomorrow." Please do not procrastinate. Start now! Feed your good habits and become aware of the habits you may not have known you had. Everything in our life is a habit: smoking, drinking, swearing, lying. We also have good habits like being a good parent, exercising, and eating healthy. It takes approximately twenty-one days to change a bad habit into a good one. Are you ready to take the challenge?We will all be somewhere in the next twenty-one days. Where will you be?

Only work on one bad habit at a time. If you have several bad habits then imagine the difference six months will make. Our life can be a very exciting story once we realize we are in control. Feeding your good habits will always bring you satisfaction and will allow you to realize you are in control of your dreams. Every habit you cultivate in your garden of life will make a difference in the lives of others. If we are struggling to move forward in life it is because we are failing to discover our inner potential. I was a street person at fifteen and a millionaire at twenty-seven. I realized my potential and shifted my bad habits into good habits in order to become who I am today. You can do the same.

Another important thing I have always lived by is knowing where we come from and never forgetting it. It is vital in understanding where we are going in the future. In all of my travels past and all of my travels in the future, I will never forget where I came from. I may have been a millionaire by the time I was twenty-seven years old but I never allowed myself to forget I was once homeless. Embrace your past and move forward because your past is what shapes you and if you know where you want to be in life, regardless of the roadblocks which may at times stall you, you will achieve your dreams. I did not live in the past but I certainly allowed my past to shape who I am today. I embrace everything life has given me and I allow roadblocks to become stepping-stones in achieving my ultimate goals. Always remember that we are responsible for our own life, therefore we cannot blame our past or others for our roadblocks. We can however, allow ourselves to learn from our past and from others in order to achieve where we would like to be in life. We are what we dream about and what we think about. I think I must be a woman. But in all seriousness, we have the power to become whatever we set our hearts on. It all begins with embracing your past and moving forward into the future.

Last but not least, having a positive attitude is an important habit to develop. Your attitude is fundamental in obtaining your goals. A person's attitude defines their mindset, their way of thinking, and their outlook on certain situations. A poor attitude will only ever result in poor results. You can regulate your life by modifying your attitude. I often like to refer to a story that I was once told about a rich boy and a poor boy. The rich child had many toys to play with. He was never deprived of anything and had the world at his fingertips. The poor boy on the other hand did not have toys to play with. He shoveled manure for fun. One day when he was asked why he continued to shovel the manure day after day, he simply responded, "With all this manure, there must be a pony somewhere."

Life is what we make of it. We must have a positive attitude in order to see the positive results in our work. Like the poor boy who shoveled manure, we mustn't complain about the work that it takes to make us successful. We must always think in terms of the end result. We must always think in terms of the pony.

Our attitude also reflects our mindset. If you are seeking the secret to success you will not find it. If you are seeking a miracle it will not happen. Your mindset is what will present you with opportunities that you may then turn into success. If you have a negative mindset, you will fail to see the right opportunities and seize them.

I always had the mindset that I was going to be successful. Even when I was living on the streets, I never viewed myself as unsuccessful. Once I became successful, I realized it was not the money that was going to make me rich it was what I was going to do with it that would have the long-term positive results. Therefore, I wanted to invest my success in personal growth and personal development. In doing so, I was investing in my future, which was a positive objective. This may seem like it is a confusing cycle but it is really quite simple. Remain positive and be persistent. When it leads you to success, use the success to invest in yourself. You will never be let down when you have a positive outlook on yourself and your future. In order to have more, you must become more. So why not invest in yourself and your future.

A very dear friend of mine once asked me, "If I walked into your house and threw garbage on your floor how would you feel?" I responded with the obvious, that it would make me very angry. He then proceeded to ask me, "Why would you allow someone to fill your mind with garbage?" It was a very good question and made me contemplate why anyone would allow their mind to become full with negativity and negative outlooks. This is simply considered garbage and should not be allowed in your mind. Opportunity will always find you if you are open-minded. Your mind is like a parachute. It works better when it is open. If you keep your mind open and free of the negativity and you may be surprised with what presents itself.

How you make your money is a reflection of who you are as a person. Money is a magnifier. It is not about how much money you have, it is about what you become as a result of it.

Chapter Eight
Life Is like an Echo

Life is like an echo. Whatever you put out into the universe you will get back. We have all heard the saying, "Sticks and stones will break my bones but names will never hurt me." I do not believe this for a second. Choose your words wisely and always be aware of what you are saying and how you are treating others around you. This begins with our children and those who look up to us. If we tell them not to smoke but we have a cigarette in our hand we are teaching them deception. If we tell them not to drink but have a drink in our hand we are teaching them hypocrisy. We need to choose our actions wisely and be aware of those around us. We should carry this lesson with us into the professional world and not allow deception and double standards to follow us into our workplace.

I once asked my grandfather why people lie and he responded in a way that I will always remember. He said I should never be disappointed in people for their negative actions. It is no mystery that people lie; that is why they are called liars. And it is no mystery that people steal; that is why they are called thieves. My grandfather explained to me that they may do these things because of the way they were brought up. We cannot be disappointed in someone for his or her actions if that is all they have ever known. What we can do is impact them in a way that will teach them to choose a positive path as opposed to the path they are engaging in.

You may be reading a lot of what I am telling you and thinking that you already know about all of this stuff. The important thing to ask yourself is if you are actually doing it. Are you making a conscious effort to change someone's life for the better? Are you trying to lead by example and show people the positive ways to achieve things in life?

A man or a woman is only as good as their word. If you are giving your word to make an effort to change the things that are negative in life and set yourself on a rewarding path then you are already well on your way to achieving happiness. How can it be that easy? You have given your word and that is the most powerful thing you can give. When people ask me the secret to my success I tell them that there are ten rules I live by. Rule number one is flawless integrity. The other nine don't matter. I truly believe that without integrity to stand on as your resolute foundation of who you are and what you do, all of the things you do and say in respect to the other nine rules will collapse.

You cannot build a skyscraper on a weak foundation. It is built one day at a time, one brick at a time. This is exactly the same as integrity. It should act as the strong foundation upon which you pave the road to your future. Integrity may be weakened at times by a little white lie or a promise to return a call that you had no intention of returning. Yes, these are considered minor infractions, however, these infractions can also be compared to a tiny trickle of water that slowly erodes the foundation of your home. It is the tiny trickle that slowly brings everything you have ever worked towards. Drop by drop, fib by fib, you are forced to repair, tear down, and rebuild your foundation. Although you may view this as an exaggerated comparison, you should not embrace it lightly. Lead with integrity and you will find that you never have to rebuild your relationships.

We are often reminded of the flaw in business in gangster movies. The line, "It's nothing personal, Vinnie, it's just business." A statement like that should be taken very personally and should never be practiced in business. Treat all relationships as personal ones and always practice integrity. It is the key to a healthy home environment as well as a healthy business environment. So ask yourself once again, do I practice integrity in my everyday life, or am I willing to sacrifice my standards for a particular outcome? While I believe in my heart of hearts that there is only one answer that should come of this question, you may be surprised by the conversation you have with yourself.

Next, you should ask yourself if the people in your life are basing their actions on a foundation of integrity. You may start to notice duplicity in your associates and colleagues. My mother used to say, "Show me your friends and I will show you your future." The same may be said of colleagues. Do not surround yourself with people who do not value integrity. This may cause a bit of a sting as you contemplate the people around you and change how you want to proceed with certain relationships. I am not saying you should cut ties with all people who seem to lack integrity. You should, however, proceed with caution. Their actions may lead you down a path of duplicity.

Has anyone ever told you they were running late? If they were running, they wouldn't be late. If someone is consistently running late then you are not that important to them and they do not respect your time. Don't be late in life.

Chapter Nine
We Are Here for a Reason

We must all believe that we were placed on this earth for a reason. Whether we have a life altering experience to realize this or whether we just know in our hearts there was a reason we were born, we all have a path in this world and we must follow that path to its end goal.

My brother and I were playing pool at a billiards hall in Vancouver, Canada when a belligerent, intoxicated man approached us. He accused me of being a police officer and soon became aggressive. To satisfy him, I finally conceded that I was a police officer. Although this was not the truth, I was hoping this would calm him down before I asked him to leave. His response was to say that he was going home to get a gun and then he stormed out of the pool hall. My brother and I had a chuckle, finished our game of pool, and then left to meet up with some friends down the street for a drink. A few minutes later we heard four gunshots ring out and in minutes the billiards hall was surrounded by police officers. The belligerent man who had gone home to get a gun was not bluffing. He returned to the pool hall and thinking that the twosome playing pool in our place were my brother and I, he shot them both. Both men died that evening and the tragedy of that event went on to follow me for a very long time. I felt that it should have been me and I felt the guilt of that for a long time. Finally I needed to follow my own advice and live without guilt. I did not die that evening for a reason. I was put on this earth for a purpose and living in the past was not going to allow me to fulfill that purpose.

I was on a pier in Canada when a large storm rolled in. A massive wave came over the pier and washed four of us into the water. We struggled to keep our heads above the water and we had no hope of swimming to shore because the undertow was too strong. That day my three companions drowned in the water. In my unconscious state I was washed up on a large board that drifted to shore. To this day I cannot explain how I became lodged on the board and ended up safely on shore.

My wife and I were planning a trip to Indonesia. We had booked our flight and made hotel reservations. The day we were to fly out, the airline informed us that they had overbooked the flight and that we were being put on standby. We went home and waited for our new flight itinerary. Two days later my wife and I were watching CNN and the hotel that we had made our reservations at had been completely destroyed in a storm. It was washed away and everyone inside the hotel lost their lives. As we watched CNN over and over again, we could not believe that an overbooked flight had prevented us from arriving at the hotel two days earlier. We were spared when so many perished.

I was in Montgomery, Mexico on a buying trip with two of my business partners. We received a warning that everyone was to evacuate the city due to devastating floods in the area. We packed up our belongings and drove for miles out of the city to higher ground. I became weary of driving, it was late in the evening, and I needed a break to relieve myself. I pulled over the car and jumped out to wander over to the side of the road for some privacy. No more than three feet in front of the car the road had been completely washed away. The current from the intense flooding and rainwater led to a two hundred foot drop. I peered over the edge to discover that not everyone has been as lucky, as we found ourselves to have stopped only moments before a deathly plummet.

When I was still living in Canada, I was coming home from work late one evening. A group of intoxicated men had stolen a car and taken a wrong turn down a one-way street. They were traveling without their headlights on and our vehicles collided head on. The men in the stolen vehicle did not make it. I survived the accident without a scratch.

I shared these stories with you, not because I wanted you to think I must be a very lucky man, but to realize that we all have a destiny and a reason for being on this earth. I am asking you to realize your path and set a goal for yourself. Envision who you want to be and know that whether you have discovered it already or not, you are meant to be someone. I survived many life and death situations that helped me to realize I had a purpose. So do you.

We've been to the moon and yet we do not take the opportunity to spend more time with the people who are important to us. It is important to prioritize in life.

Chapter Ten

I Love You Too, Mr. Mercer

Have you ever seen a Brinks truck following a hearse? When someone passes away, it's often asked how much money did someone leave behind. They left it all behind. So why not use our money to help others? I spent the first half of my life making money. I intend to spend the second half of my life spending it on things that matter. Why not leave a legacy? It will mean so much more than the money.

My brother was twelve when he was diagnosed with leukemia. He did not beat leukemia but he also did not leave us with a single ounce of negativity. He was strong and he embraced life to the fullest. He never allowed people to see his pain or his fear, he wanted people to see how happy he was with the way he was leaving this earth. He was in the hospital for eighty days before he passed away. I was there for all eighty days. My brother forced me to realize that everything happens for a reason and circumstances in life present themselves so that we can make the most of what we are given.

The day my brother passed on he said one of the most profound things anyone has ever said to me. To this day it rings clear in my head and it effects all of the decisions I make. My brother said to me, "God is going to take me away today but I want you to know that if I was to grow up as an adult, I would want to be just like you." I knew at that moment that I was put here for a reason and I have dedicated the rest of my life to helping others and being an influence to others the same way that I was to my brother.

There was a young boy in the same ward of the hospital as my brother. His name was Arnie and he was inflicted with several diseases, one which left him unable to speak. His parents did not have a lot of money, not even enough to come and visit them as much as they would like. Arnie was also a huge sports fanatic and his parents were unable to afford a television for him so I arranged for a TV to be brought into his room. I bought him a sticker book and would bring him sports stickers. He was elated and although he could not speak, I knew he was thankful. Everyday when I left the hospital I would poke my head into Arnie's room and say, "I love you,

Arnie." He would smile back at me with a beam that could melt an iceberg.

On the very last day of Arnie's life I did as I always did. I poked my head into Arnie's room and said, "I love you, Arnie." As plain as day Arnie looked back at me and said, "I love you too, Mr. Mercer."

We must all realize that we are all here for a reason. No matter how big or small we have the power to impact the people around us. I had the opportunity to impact my brother and Arnie in a way that mattered most to them. Make it your goal to positively impact those around you. Your own unique way of impacting others is what will be most profound. Whether it is being a mentor to your younger sibling or purchasing stickers for a child who may not be able to afford them otherwise, our actions are powerful.

In hindsight, I realize my brother passed away with no regrets. He embraced what he was given and passed away peacefully knowing he had given life his all. If more people led by his example we would have such a powerful planet. Live life without regrets and without guilt. You may be saying, "Well, Mr. Mercer, this is far easier said than done," but I know you can do it. Always act in a manner of knowing that what you are doing is right. If you always know what you are doing is the right thing then you will never have any regrets or guilt because you did the right thing. If you make a mistake then look back and ask yourself if you have learned something from the mistake. If so, you have no regrets. If not, you need to look harder to see the lesson in your mistake.

Do not stop doing the things that bring

you joy and laughter in life. Find

something that you are passionate about

and build on it.

Chapter Eleven
Impactful Stories

I come from a family of five male children. My youngest brother died of leukemia when he was twelve. My next brother killed himself in a drunk driving accident after drinking two bottles of vodka. My third brother also died from alcohol abuse. I have not seen or heard from my fourth brother in many years. I am not sure if he is dead or alive. I have experienced my fair share of tragedy. I have never felt sorry for myself and I have never allowed tragedy to damper my outlook on life. We all have the ability to become successful regardless of the circumstances in our life. I have always had my eyes wide open and I have come to realize the reasons for success or failure.

When you compare average people with the people who have obtained far more success in life, it is easy to see where the average person went wrong. Average people dip their toes in the water. Successful people jump right in and immerse themselves. Average people avoid failure by never challenging themselves whereas successful people embrace failure as part of their success. You must distinguish yourself from the average in order to become successful. It is never beneficial to view yourself as above anyone else, however knowing what you want and distinguishing yourself from the people who do not will become very important in your life journey.

Welcome to the top 3 percent! A study done at Yale University revealed that only 3 percent of all graduating seniors actually had written goals and plans on how to achieve them. If you begin writing down your goals and moving forward on a plan of action to achieve them you will be among a special 3 percent of people. You have to know what you want in life. Many people know what they don't want, but they are unsure of what they do want in life. Set your goals based on what you do want in life and you will become successful. My question to you is, why do so many people realize the importance of goal setting and yet they fail to write their own goals down? Do not fall into this group. Be a part of the successful people who write down their goals and seek to achieve them with every decision they make in life.

A friend of mine was complaining about her aches and pains. How her eyesight was going and her hearing seemed to be deteriorating. I smiled at her and told her not to worry, who wants to live to be 100 years old anyways? She looked at me and with conviction in her voice she responded, "Someone who is ninety-nine years old." My friend made me realize we all need to live life to the fullest and that wishing away our years is pointless and will never get us anywhere. We cannot take life for granted or it will pass us by. We may think we do not want to live until we cannot see or hear as well as we once could but if you said that to a ninety-nine year old person, you want to bet they would want to live that extra year.

On the topic of being elderly and looking after ourselves, an older man went to see his doctor for his annual physical exam. His doctor looked him over and observed that he was in tremendous shape. "How old are you again?" he asked. "I'm eighty-eight years old," the man replied. The doctor inquired as to how his patient was able to stay in such great shape. "Well, you see, doctor, my wife and I made a pact that whenever she got angry with me she would go into the kitchen and I would go outside to cool down." Confused the doctor asked what that had to do with anything. The patient sighed, "I have lived outdoors pretty much all of my life." I just thought I would throw in another one of my funny little zingers to make sure I still have your attention.

This chapter focuses on stories that have impacted me in a big way. A long time ago I came across a story in the newspaper that changed my outlook on life, about money in particular. It took place in Florida. Three patients from a disability hospital purchased a lottery ticket. They won twenty-seven million dollars. The first of the excited winners was a woman who had been blinded by a bad accident. She was married with two children. When she was asked what she would do with the money, without hesitation she said, "If only I could see my husband and my two children I would give away my nine million." The second winner was deaf and unable to speak. Through sign language he communicated that if he regained his hearing and learned to speak he would give up his nine million. The final winner in the group was confined to a wheel chair. He knew immediately that with his nine million dollars he would like to be able to walk again.

When I heard this story I was impacted in a big way. I can talk, hear, see, and walk and none of these things cost me a penny. Right there on the spot I felt as though I had a net worth of twenty-seven million dollars. That in itself made me realize that I am incredibly wealthy and no amount of success would equal that what was given to me by God.

Another inspiring story that I once came across involved a man who had a lot of work to do one evening to prepare for a major project. His son, however, wanted his father's attention and although the man loved his son very much, the project was incredibly important. The father did not want to hurt his son's feelings so he came up with a brilliant idea. Beside him lay the daily newspaper and in the center of the paper there was a large map of the world that was being used to advertise a travel agency. The father took the picture of the map and ripped it up into many pieces. He gave it to his son with a roll of tape. He said, "I want to see how smart you are. Let's see how long it will take you to put the map of the world back together."

The father anticipated that this would take his young son many hours and by the time his son was finished, he would be done his project. About five minutes later the little boy handed the completed map of the world to his father. Amazed and completely awe struck, the father could not believe how quickly his son completed the map. He asked his son how he managed to get it done so quickly and the young boy simply responded, "Daddy, on the opposite side of the map of the world there was a picture of a man. Once the man was together, the world was together."

The young boy had taken the complexity of the map of the world and simplified it by understanding that the picture on the back would lead him to the same end goal. His father failed to see the simplicity in the task. Sometimes we need to stop and reconsider our tasks at hand. Standing back, understanding our task and tackling it from a different perspective will oftentimes lead us to positive results we are seeking.

Your comfort zone is a direct reflection of the balance of your bank account. Take risks in life. Time is all we have. Use it wisely.

Chapter Twelve

Small Gestures Can Make a World of Difference

I want to share a story with you that deserves a chapter of its own. It is this story that made me realize we truly do not know why some people end up in the unfortunate circumstances life gives them, however we all have the ability to overcome those circumstances regardless of why we end up in them. Take myself for instance. I was homeless at a very young age. I did not have family or friends to take me in and give me a foot up in life. I was responsible for my own future and I choose to pave a successful path for myself as opposed to a life on the streets. The story I am about to share with you will hopefully open your eyes to the fact that no matter what our life circumstance may be, we all have the ability to change our circumstances and we are the only ones responsible for choosing to make something more of our lives.

I was in Miami doing a seminar and decided to go for a walk between sessions. I walked past a beggar in the street who shouted at me, "Nice Italian shoes." I paid no mind to him and continued walking until I heard him yell out, "Nice Versace suit." This caught my attention, as many people would not be able to discern between a Versace suit and a regular suit. I turned around and walked back towards him to ask him how he knew it was a Versace suit. He proceeded to tell me that he worked at Versace for many years as the head of security. This was hard to believe coming from a man who smelt and was badly beaten up. He had one eye half closed and scratches all over his face. It was hard to believe he had once held a coveted position at the Versace fashion house. He went on to explain that some thugs had beaten him up the night before and had also broken his glasses. Feeling pity for him, I walked over to a Walgreens and purchased some bottles of water and some sandwiches, gauze, and rubbing alcohol as well as a pair of reading glasses. I also gave him twenty dollars.

A few days later I walked past the same spot where I had found this man earlier in the week. However, the man who was sitting there this time was barely recognizable. To this day, picturing the transformation of this man brings tears to my eyes. He had gone to a shelter to have a shower and had gotten his hair cut. He had bought a clean shirt, pants, and shoes from the Salvation Army and although they did not ask for money from him, he made a ten-dollar donation. He reached into his pocket and handed me the other ten-dollar bill. Of course, I did not take it but it certainly earned him a lot of respect in my book.

The next day I found this man sitting outside of my hotel room. I had the day off so I asked him if he would like to join me for a few rounds of pool at a local billiard place. I ordered up a beer and he declined my offer of a beer explaining that he had quit drinking. When I asked him when, he simply smiled and responded, "Yesterday." He said that because of me, he had decided to turn his life around. This poor man sat in the same spot and regardless of the fact that is was an affluent part of Miami, it was between Christmas and New Years and he was lucky if he was given one dollar. He said that small children would spit at him and others would take pictures. Young men coming out of the bars would often urinate on him for fun. This was no life for a man who once held a respected position at Versace. He explained that after Versace was killed he lost his job as head of security. Shortly after, his wife and three children were coming home from church when a drunk driver drove over the median and hit his family head on. His wife and one child died instantly. His other two children struggled on life support before also passing away. Their medical bills were very expensive which ultimately led to him losing his house. When I asked him why he chose the streets over a shelter, he simply said that the shelter was only concerned with speaking about God. He explained to me that he had lost his faith when he lost his family.

I continued to meet up with this man for lengthy conversations and one day he was rather excited to tell me that he had gotten a job parking cars and his employer had also offered him a place to live. He invited me over to see his new living quarters. It was a basement apartment with a fridge and stove, a clean bed, and a washroom. It was a pleasant place to stay and it gave him a foot up in the world to begin his new life. I assisted him in giving him a new beginning. We all have the power to help others who are in need. So the next time you walk by a homeless person do not assume that they are in this position because they will not find work or they have taken to drugs and alcohol. We all come from different walks of life and, sometimes, hearing someone out and helping them where you can will make all the difference.

You cannot make sense out of nonsense.

Integrity will bring you credibility. It is

time for you to make a positive difference.

Chapter Thirteen

I Can Almost Touch Heaven from Here

In 1987 my wife and I decided to go on a vacation to Costa Rica. I have changed her name in this chapter to Karen for privacy reasons, however all accounts in this chapter continue to be as true as the rest of this book. I have to admit the idea to visit Costa Rica was entirely Karen's idea. She had a vision in mind that I simply assisted her in achieving. When we arrived in Costa Rica we met with a man who only had two horses, however, he wanted to show Karen some waterfalls so I allowed them to venture on without me. I waited for them at the bottom of the mountain and as I waited I saw eagles, monkeys, toucans, parrots, humming birds, butterflies, and multitudes of other wildlife. I suddenly had my eyes opened to the tremendous beauty the country of Costa Rica had to offer. I was overwhelmed and awestruck by what I had seen in a few short hours.

Karen returned from her journey up the mountain and asked me how I liked Costa Roca so far. I turned to her and said, "I am not sure if I will ever make it to heaven but I can almost touch it from here." It was from that moment on that there was no turning back. We decided to set up life in Costa Rica and we have been there ever since.

We ended up purchasing the property on the mountain that the man had taken her to see. At first I questioned her sanity as I certainly loved Costa Rica but did not understand her vision at the time. Over the years her vision became apparent to me and purchasing property in Costa Rica became the best investment we ever made.

I became attached to the country of Costa Rica in heart and mind. I had my eyes opened to tremendous beauty and serenity and yet there were still negatives in what I thought to be paradise. People were stealing the scarlet macaw and sometimes even killing them to sell their beautiful feathers. There were also thousands of turtle eggs being stolen and sold illegally as an aphrodisiac. Wealthy people were purchasing monkeys to own as pets. It became apparent to me that the very reason Costa Rica was so beautiful was also the cause for much corruption and illegal activity. This is when I became heavily involved in philanthropy. Karen and I spent millions of dollars of our own money on purchasing an island to preserve the wildlife of Costa Rica. We planted hundreds of trees and hired armed guards to protect the island from thieves looking to steal the seas turtles and monkeys for sale in illegal market.

Money should never be measured by how much you have but rather by what you do with it once you have it. Karen and I devoted much of our time to protecting the wildlife of Costa Rica. I came to realize that having money for self-gain is never as rewarding as having money to make a difference in the lives of others. I have traveled all over North America to talk about environmental issues and because of my efforts I was inducted into the Environmental Hall of Fame in 2008.

I have been truly blessed by the people I have met in my life and each and every person I meet becomes a powerful encounter that shapes who I am. My mother used to tell me to never speak to strangers, but strangers are the only friends I have ever met. Karen was once a stranger to me and without her I never would have come to develop a life in Costa Rica. She had a vision and she made her dream come true. It is because of this I came to protect the Costa Rican wildlife, be inducted into the

Environmental Hall of Fame, and ultimately touch the lives of many around me.

Vision is everything. When I was poor and living on the streets at fifteen years old, I did not view myself as poor. I viewed myself as fortunate to be alive and to have what I did. A friend of mine from years ago came to visit my wife and me. When he saw our home he said he would have hated to pay the property taxes and that the pool must cost a fortune to keep up. I smiled at him and said he was lucky he did not have to be concerned with such matters. On the other hand I thought his situation was quite unfortunate because he obviously never envisioned himself as living an expensive lifestyle. You have to have a vision of what you want to obtain and a goal to achieve it before you can accomplish it.

I have been to eighty-six countries, every single state in the United States, and every province in Canada and yet I choose to call Costa Rica my home. I truly consider Costa Rica to be the most peaceful and pleasant place in the world. I live on a property where I raise my own free-range chickens. I have a vast orchard that grows mangoes and oranges, avocadoes, bananas, star fruit, and grapefruit. I revere the level of life to be of the highest standing in Costa Rica because you live among nature and have the ability to harvest your own crops and grow your own fruit and vegetables all the while enjoying the wildlife that stands at your very doorstep.

This book is not intended to be a motivational book that will give you the answers to all of the pitfalls you may face in life. It's simply designed to get you thinking about what you what out of life and how to begin your journey of achieving your goals. It includes inspiring stories throughout the chapters to help you reflect when times get tough.

I was living on the streets as a young teen. I have an eighth grade eight education yet I was able to alter my life path for the better. I am now a successful businessman and philanthropist. I own property in Costa Rica and pride myself in helping others. This book is intended to help people to realize that no matter what life throws at you, you are in control of the outcome and you and only you are responsible for getting what you want out of life.

Use a felt tip marker. Underline the stories that are meaningful to you. Reflect on them and write down your own inspirational stories. Talk to people in the streets, take a moment out of your day to realize your dreams, and align your path with obtaining them. Reread this book and always keep in mind that we are in control of our future. Choose to make it a successful one.

Made in the USA
Charleston, SC
11 May 2016